How to cultivate personal well-being

Personal development guide for a happy and fulfilled life

Jane Hawkins

SUMMARY

<u>CHAPTER 1: INTRODUCTION TO PERSONAL WELL-BEING</u>

Personal well-being is a very important concept and it is important to understand how to take better care of oneself and one's needs.

Personal well-being can be defined as the feeling of security and satisfaction in one's personal and professional life, respect for oneself and others, and the ability to achieve goals.

It is also a state of mind that enables a person to live a fulfilling and harmonious personal life and to maintain good mental and physical health.

This guide provides an introduction to the concept of personal well-being and its various aspects.

Personal well-being is a concept that covers many areas and can be approached from many different angles.

It is important to understand these different domains and how they can interconnect and contribute to a state of personal well-being.

First, it is important to understand what personal well-being means.

Personal well-being can include feeling secure and satisfied in one's personal and professional life, respect for oneself and others, and the ability to achieve goals.

It can also include such things as feeling safe in one's home and environment, feeling secure and stable in one's relationships with others, being able to express oneself and communicate, and being able to make healthy and responsible decisions.

Personal well-being is closely linked to physical and mental health.

Physical health is an important component of personal wellness and includes such things as nutrition, exercise and healthy lifestyle habits.

Mental health is also important and can include things such as treatment for depression, anxiety and other mental disorders.

These two aspects of personal wellness are closely related and understanding them can help improve both and maintain a state of personal wellness.

Personal well-being can also be linked to a number of social skills.

These skills can include things like the ability to communicate and express feelings, the ability to form healthy relationships, and the ability to adapt to new situations.

These skills are essential to maintaining good personal well-being.

Personal well-being is also linked to a number of other factors such as stress management, time management and financial management.

Stress management is important because it can help reduce stress levels and manage stress more effectively.

Time management is also important because it can help a person successfully balance their personal and professional life and find time to take care of themselves and their loved ones.

Financial management is also important because it can help one set financial goals and achieve them.

Introduction to personal wellness is a very important topic and it is important to understand these different aspects and how they can interact to create a state of personal wellness.

Understanding personal wellness can help improve physical and mental health and maintain a fulfilling and harmonious personal life.

CHAPTER 2: UNDERSTANDING YOUR MINDSET

In a world filled with stress and pressure, understanding your state of mind can be one of the most important ways to cultivate personal well-being.

People tend to be stressed and anxious because of the pressures of life, and this can have detrimental effects on their physical and mental health.

It is important to understand how your state of mind affects your life, and how you can constructively manage these pressures and feelings.

One of the most useful tools to better understand your state of mind is meditation.

Meditation can help calm thoughts and emotions and connect with your mind and body.

It is a practice that can be very beneficial to your mental and physical health.

Meditation can help you feel calmer and better understand your thoughts and emotions.

It can also help you better manage stress and anxiety.

Another way to understand your state of mind is to use mindfulness techniques.

Mindfulness is about being fully aware and accepting thoughts and emotions without judgment.

Practicing mindfulness can help you develop a better understanding of your state of mind and how it affects your life.

Another way to understand your state of mind is to take time to reflect on your thoughts and emotions.

Taking time to reflect on how you feel can help you develop a better understanding of what is going on in your mind.

It can also be helpful to think about how you react to situations and people.

This can help you better understand why you react in certain ways and find ways to handle situations with more calm and equanimity.

Another way to improve your state of mind is to find ways to relax and unwind.

Relaxation can be a very effective way to reduce stress and anxiety and help you better manage your thoughts and emotions.

There are many ways to relax, such as yoga, meditation, reading, writing, gardening, walking, etc.

Finding activities that help you feel calm and better manage your thoughts and emotions can be very beneficial.

Finally, another way to understand your state of mind is to take the time to discuss your thoughts and emotions with a friend or family member.

Taking the time to discuss what is going on in your mind and talk about how you feel can help you develop a better understanding of your thoughts and emotions.

It can also help you find ways to better manage pressure and anxiety.

Understanding your state of mind and finding ways to better manage thoughts and emotions is essential to cultivating personal well-being.

Meditation, mindfulness, reflection and relaxation are tools that can help you better understand your state of mind and find ways to better manage stress and anxiety.

It is also important to take the time to discuss your thoughts and emotions with a friend or family member.

By taking the time to understand and manage your state of mind, you will be able to better cultivate personal well-being.

<u>**CHAPTER 3: DEVELOP YOUR SELF-CONFIDENCE**</u>

Self-confidence is one of the main keys to personal well-being.

A person who feels secure and confident in their abilities is more likely to take risks and pursue their dreams.

However, self-confidence is not something we can acquire overnight.

It takes time and dedication to learn to appreciate ourselves and feel comfortable with our imperfections.

Fortunately, there are ways to develop our self-confidence and achieve personal well-being.

The first step in developing your self-confidence is to accept yourself as you are.

This starts with recognizing our qualities and imperfections and being willing to accept them.

You will never be perfect, and that is perfectly normal.

Learning to accept your physical appearance and character traits will help you feel more comfortable in your own skin and build your confidence.

Another way to build your confidence is to take the time to surround yourself with positive people.

When you are surrounded by supportive and encouraging people, it can have a significant impact on your confidence.

Don't hesitate to listen to their advice and let them help you feel better about yourself.

Finally, you can build your confidence by taking small steps toward your goals.

Whether it's learning a new skill or reaching your career goals, it's important to give yourself achievable goals and reach them.

This will help you feel more capable and confident in your abilities.

Ultimately, it is important to remember that self-confidence is something we need to cultivate every day.

Take the time to accept yourself and surround yourself with positive people, and take small steps to achieve your goals.

With time and hard work, you will find that your confidence grows and you begin to feel better about yourself.

<u>**CHAPTER 4: GET TO KNOW YOURSELF**</u>

Personal well-being is an important aspect of life.

It is important to take the time to get to know yourself.

It can help you better understand who you are and what you want in life.

Getting to know yourself can be a process that can take some time, but it is well worth it.

There are several ways to start getting to know yourself.

One of the first steps is to take some time to reflect and think about who you are.

A good way to do this is to get a notebook and start writing.

You could write about what you like, what you want in life and what is important to you.

You can also write about your aspirations, dreams and goals.

Another way to get to know yourself is to look back and think about your life journey.

You might ask yourself what motivated you to make certain decisions, and how those decisions have affected your life.

You could also look at some of the difficult times you've been through and see how you managed to overcome them.

Another way to learn about yourself is to connect with your emotions and feelings.

Take time to think about how you feel and why you are feeling that way.

You might ask yourself why you are happy, sad, angry, anxious or nervous.

Take time to connect with how you feel and see if you can find a way to manage your emotions more effectively.

Another way to get to know yourself is to start exploring your beliefs and values.

You might want to take some time to think about what you believe and why you believe it.

You could also reflect on what is important to you and why it is important.

Take time to connect with your beliefs and values and see how these things might help you feel better.

Finally, getting to know yourself can also mean taking time to understand who you are and what you want in life.

You could take time to think about what you want in life and what you want to accomplish.

You could also reflect on what is important to you and what you really want in life.

Take time to better understand who you are and what you want and see how these things can help you cultivate personal well-being.

Getting to know yourself is an important part of the personal wellness process.

Take time to reflect on who you are and what you want in life.

Take time to understand your emotions, beliefs and values.

Take time to explore your life journey and see how these things can help you cultivate personal wellness.

Take time to know yourself and see how that can help you cultivate personal well-being.

<u>CHAPTER 5: LEARN TO COMMUNICATE WITH OTHERS</u>

Empathy is one of the most important qualities for personal well-being.

It is defined as the ability to perceive and understand the emotions and feelings of others.

But how can you develop your empathy to better understand others and find personal happiness?

First of all, it is important to understand that empathy is not something you can develop overnight.

It takes work and patience to fully integrate into your life.

Start by getting to know yourself and identifying your own emotions and feelings.

Take time to observe and reflect on what is going on in your body, your mood and your thoughts.

This will help you better understand and manage your emotions.

Next, learn to observe others and read their expressions and gestures.

Try to understand what is going on with others and how they react to certain situations.

This will help you better understand their emotions and feelings.

Finally, learn to listen to others and give them your attention.

Listen to them with empathy and without judgment and try to understand their points of view and perspectives.

This will help you better understand their intentions and connect with them.

Cultivating empathy takes time and practice, but it's a skill that can help you better communicate with others and find happiness.

Empathy can also help you better understand yourself and your own emotions and feelings.

Take time to practice listening and observing others and trying to understand their views and perspectives.

Listen with empathy and without judgment and try to understand their intentions.

This will help you better understand their emotions and feelings and learn to better communicate and respond to others.

Cultivating empathy is a skill that can help you better understand others and find personal happiness.

Take the time to learn more about yourself, observe others and listen to their views and perspectives.

This will help you better understand their emotions and feelings and respond better to others.

CHAPTER 6: LEARN TO MANAGE YOUR EMOTIONS

Personal well-being is a very important topic, as it can have a huge impact on your quality of life and your ability to succeed in various fields.

Therefore, learning to manage your emotions is one of the most important elements of your personal well-being.

This chapter will explain how you can learn to manage your emotions and use them to your advantage.

First, it is important to understand what emotions are and how they work.

Emotions are physiological and psychological responses to a given situation.

They are usually triggered by external factors, such as events or people, or by internal thoughts, such as memories or beliefs.

Each emotion has its own set of physical and psychological manifestations.

For example, fear is usually accompanied by a feeling of muscle tension, an increased heart rate and a feeling of cold.

Similarly, anger is usually accompanied by a feeling of heat, increased blood pressure and a feeling of tightness.

It is important to remember that all emotions are normal and necessary responses to specific situations.

Once you understand how your emotions work, you can begin to learn how to manage them.

Emotion management techniques may vary depending on the individual and the specific situation.

However, there are some general strategies that can be helpful.

The first is to practice mindfulness.

Mindfulness is a state of mind in which you are aware of your thoughts, feelings and sensations.

By practicing mindfulness, you will learn to recognize and accept your emotions without judgment and step back from them.

You can then decide whether or not you want to respond to your emotion.

You can also use relaxation techniques, such as meditation or yoga, to help you calm down and better manage your emotions.

Another way to learn how to manage your emotions is to understand what causes them.

For example, if you feel anxious about a situation, you can take the time to look at the situation and determine what is causing your anxiety.

By doing this, you can find ways to stop your emotional reactions.

You can also learn to manage your emotions by developing your ability to communicate.

By talking about your emotions with someone you trust, you can better understand them and learn to manage them.

If you are not comfortable with this, you can always consult a psychologist or therapist who can help you understand and manage your emotions.

Finally, you can also learn to manage your emotions by setting boundaries.

Learn to say no and protect yourself from situations that are too emotionally intense for you.

Learn to step back and walk away from situations that are too difficult to handle.

Learning to manage your emotions can take time and effort.

However, by developing your emotional management skills, you can improve your personal well-being and your ability to succeed in a variety of areas.

By taking the time to get to know yourself and learn to manage your emotions, you can feel calmer, more balanced and happier.

CHAPTER 7: DEVELOP YOUR EMPATHY

Empathy is one of the most important qualities for personal well-being.

It is defined as the ability to perceive and understand the emotions and feelings of others.

But how can you develop your empathy to better understand others and find personal happiness?

First of all, it is important to understand that empathy is not something you can develop overnight.

It takes work and patience to fully integrate into your life.

Start by getting to know yourself and identifying your own emotions and feelings.

Take time to observe and reflect on what is going on in your body, your mood and your thoughts.

This will help you better understand and manage your emotions.

Next, learn to observe others and read their expressions and gestures.

Try to understand what is going on with others and how they react to certain situations.

This will help you better understand their emotions and feelings.

Finally, learn to listen to others and give them your attention.

Listen to them with empathy and without judgment and try to understand their points of view and perspectives.

This will help you better understand their intentions and connect with them.

Cultivating empathy takes time and practice, but it's a skill that can help you better communicate with others and find happiness.

Empathy can also help you better understand yourself and your own emotions and feelings.

Take time to practice listening and observing others and trying to understand their views and perspectives.

Listen with empathy and without judgment and try to understand their intentions.

This will help you better understand their emotions and feelings and learn to better communicate and respond to others.

Cultivating empathy is a skill that can help you better understand others and find personal happiness.

Take the time to learn more about yourself, observe others and listen to their views and perspectives.

This will help you better understand their emotions and feelings and respond better to others.

CHAPTER 8: BUILDING SELF-ESTEEM

You are more than what others think of you.

You are more than what you are today. You have the ability to improve yourself, to surpass yourself and to rise higher.

You are the only person who can develop your self-esteem and personal well-being.

Self-esteem is a positive perception you have of yourself.

It is deeply rooted in you and manifests itself in your sense of self-worth and your ability to succeed.

Self-esteem is essential to happiness and satisfaction in life.

Developing your own self-esteem is a long process.

It is important to know your own strengths and weaknesses and to accept them.

This means that you must learn to love yourself for who you are and accept your flaws and limitations.

You must also give yourself the same respect that you give to others.

The first step in developing your self-esteem is to do an honest and realistic self-assessment of yourself.

Take time to reflect on your life and what you have accomplished and what you want to accomplish.

Think about the positive things you have accomplished and what makes you unique.

Take time to acknowledge and learn from your mistakes.

Once you have done the self-assessment, you need to make changes in your attitude and behavior.

Once you have accepted your strengths and weaknesses, you can begin to work on your flaws and turn them into strengths.

This can be done by adopting positive attitudes and making informed decisions.

To develop your self-esteem and personal well-being, you must also learn to set achievable goals and reach them.

This can be done by setting realistic goals and working hard to achieve them.

You must also learn to accept your failures and learn from your mistakes.

Another way to build your self-esteem is to surround yourself with positive and encouraging people.

You need to surround yourself with people who support and encourage you to achieve your goals and fulfill your potential.

You must also learn to say no to people and things that hurt you.

You also need to learn to manage your emotions.

This can be done by taking time to think about your feelings and put them into words.

You also need to take time to relax and unwind.

Activities such as meditation and mindfulness can help you manage your emotions and feel better.

Finally, you need to learn to trust yourself.

You must learn to make decisions and trust your intuition.

You also need to learn to accept your inability to make decisions sometimes.

Self-confidence is essential for personal well-being and life satisfaction.

In summary, developing your self-esteem is a long-term process and it is important to take the time to do an honest and realistic self-assessment of yourself.

You must also learn to accept your strengths and weaknesses and work on your flaws.

You must also learn to surround yourself with positive people and manage your emotions.

Finally, you must learn to trust yourself and accept your mistakes.

CHAPTER 9: LEARN TO MAKE DECISIONS

Personal wellness is a process of personal development and growth that requires you to make decisions for yourself and your future.

Decision-making is an important aspect of personal wellness and can be a complex and difficult process.

Making decisions can be stressful and scary, but understanding how to make decisions for your own personal well-being is crucial.

Decision making begins with identifying your goals and values.

It is important to ensure that your goals and values are clearly defined and that you are aware of what is important to you.

You also need to be aware of the potential consequences of your decision and ensure that you are able to manage those consequences.

Once you have identified your goals and values, you need to take the time to consider all the options available to you that align with your goals and values.

It is important to consider the strengths and weaknesses of each option and to make sure you consider all the factors that could influence your decision.

You also need to consider the potential consequences of your decision and make sure that you are able to manage those consequences.

Once you have considered all the options and consequences, you need to make a final decision.

Once you have made your decision, it is important to take time to reflect on your choices and to take time to plan your next step.

It is important to remember that you have the right to change your mind and make different decisions as your life evolves.

It is also important to remember that the decisions we make can have consequences and that you must be prepared to deal with the consequences.

It is also important to remember that the decision-making process can sometimes take time.

Don't be afraid to take the time you need to consider all the options and think about the potential consequences of your decision.

Take the time to weigh the pros and cons and make a decision that will help you achieve your goals and cultivate your personal well-being.

It is also important to recognize that no one can make the decisions for you.

You must be willing to take risks and accept the consequences of your decisions.

You must also be willing to question yourself and take time to reflect on your decisions to ensure that you are able to make them with confidence and wisdom.

Decision-making is an important aspect of personal well-being and can be a complex and difficult process.

It is important to take the time to reflect on your goals and values, consider all options and their consequences, and make a final decision.

You must also be willing to accept the consequences of your decision and take time to reflect on your choices.

Making decisions can seem difficult and scary, but it can be an important step in cultivating personal well-being.

CHAPTER 10: LEARN TO RELAX

Personal well-being is a matter of choice.

You can choose to live a healthy, balanced life filled with moments of relaxation and enjoyment.

Relaxation is an essential part of personal wellness and can help you manage stress and better handle difficult situations.

In this chapter, we will teach you how to relax and feel better in your body and mind.

First, become aware of your body and your feelings.

You can do this by sitting or walking.

Focus on your breathing and notice how your body responds to your breathing.

Take time to acknowledge and accept the feelings that are occurring.

Then try to refocus on yourself and move away from thoughts that stress you out.

Notice all the little positive things that are happening in your life and focus on them.

You can also imagine yourself in a quiet, peaceful place, such as a garden or a beach, and take time to relax.

Once you are in a calmer state, you can focus on your body and relax it.

You can start with breathing techniques, such as yoga or meditation.

You can also do stretching or muscle relaxation exercises.

These techniques will help you release the tension that builds up in your body.

You can also try softer ways to relax, such as listening to relaxing music, taking a warm bath, reading a book or taking a walk.

These activities can help you relax and refocus on yourself.

If you are really stressed, you can try more advanced relaxation techniques, such as hypnosis or EFT (Emotional Freedom Technique).

These techniques can help you relax and manage your thoughts and emotions.

Finally, take the time to listen to yourself and respect yourself.

Set realistic goals for yourself and don't let the difficulties overwhelm you.

Learn to tell yourself that everything will be okay and to give yourself time to rest and relax.

These tips will help you learn to relax and cultivate personal well-being.

Take the time to practice these techniques and you will see your stress levels decrease and your well-being improve.

<u>WHO IS JANE HAWKINS?</u>

Jane Hawkins is a prolific and passionate author who began writing at the age of 17.

She has published more than 100 books in a variety of genres, ranging from fiction to personal development.

She is known for her unique and interesting style, and her books are read by people all over the world.

Her passion for writing is what drives her every day and she writes in both French and English.

Her words are captivating and her stories are full of inspiration and emotion.

She loves to share her passion for literature with her readers, and offer them new perspectives.

If you have enjoyed a Jane Hawkins book, please leave her a positive review on Amazon!

<u>Notes :</u>

....

....

....

....

....

....

....

....

....

....

....

....

....

....

....

....

....

....

....

....